The story of the Washington family begins with William, who settled at Washington in north-east England before 1180; but his forebears may be traced for many generations.

William's parents, Sir Patric, second son of Earl Gospatric III of Dunbar (who died in 1166) and his wife Cicely, appear with their son in a list of benefactors of Durham Priory.

From his grandmother, the pious Countess Dierdre, who, with her husband Earl Gospatric, founded the nunnery of Coldstream, William inherited the Border estate of the Hirsel (today the seat of the Douglas-Home family, also descendants of Earl Gospatric) and lands at Greenlaw nearby.

The earls of Dunbar held extensive estates both in north-east and north-west England, including the barony of Beanley in Northumberland, besides being tenants of Milburn, not far distant in Westmorland (Cumbria). Patric, William's father, seems to have held Helsington, Westmorland, under William of Lancaster, lord of Kendal; and from this period members of the Washington family appear frequently in Kendal records. The descent of the family properties in Berwickshire, Northumberland, Durham and Westmorland, appears to have been well established before William settled at Washington and adopted its name, explaining the early and continuing connections of the family with these widespread areas.

Like other great medieval landed proprietors, the Washingtons moved between their estates, living in different properties in turn while performing local duties and services, but known by the name of their principal residence.

William, descended from the younger son of an ancient noble house, became the founder of another great line which, after varied fortunes, produced the first President of the United States of America.

Washington Old Hall today. The south front faces the former courtyard, now gardens. Cottages on the left were rebuilt from former stables and the lodgings of footmen who, in medieval times, would fight for their lord. The house, although extensively rebuilt about 1623, incorporates medieval masonry. National Trust property and open to visitors April–October. For further details, contact the Administrator. Tel. 091–4166879.

Margot Johnson.

The Washingtons of Washington

The Washingtons took their name from a parish in the old County Palatine of Durham in north-east England. Wessyngton, variously spelled, and Washington today, lies north of the River Wear on a tidal stretch a few miles upstream from Monkwearmouth (now part of Sunderland), where the Venerable Bede became a monk in the seventh century.

WILLIAM DE WESSYNGTON, the first of the family to bear the name, was the son of the Berwickshire thegn, Sir Patric of *Le Hirsell,* a Scottish estate on the Tweed. Sir Patric held also Offerton across the Wear from Washington and his son William was the tenant of Hartburn, further south in County Durham.

As William de Hertburn, he exchanged Hertburn (now Hartburn) for Washington, which became his principal residence a little before 1180. It was natural for him to assume 'de Wessyngton' as his new name. Surnames as we now know them had not yet developed. Both places were part of the estates of the bishops of Durham, who exercised a three-fold role: first, as bishops of a great diocese stretching from the River Tees to the Scottish Border; second, as owners of vast estates covering the whole of the old county of Durham (the lands between Tyne and Tees) as well as others in Yorkshire and elsewhere; and third, as counts palatine, holding vice-regal powers and with responsibilities for defending the Scottish borders.

Bishop Hugh of Le Puiset (1153–95), nephew of King Stephen, able administrator and great builder, reorganised the bishopric estates and developed new towns. At Stockton-on-Tees, he built a new fortified manor house and wanted Hartburn to round out the property. It was convenient for William to relinquish it in exchange for Washington because of its closeness to Offerton, to which he was heir.

About 1182, he married the young twice-widowed Countess Margaret, his kinswoman and younger sister of William the Lion, King of Scotland. She was first married to Conan *le Petit,* Earl of Richmond and Duke of Brittany, who died in 1171; and afterwards to Humphrey de Bohun who died in 1181. In 1184 she is recorded as holding unspecified lands in Westmorland.

Washington Old Hall. West end of the great hall with part of the former screens passage. The two arches, part of the fourteenth-century house where William de Wessyngton's descendants lived until 1452, led from the screens passage to the buttery and pantry, converted to a kitchen in the seventeenth century. The medieval kitchen, now gone, lay beyond.
Tyne and Wear County Council.

William de Wessyngton had four children, evidently by an earlier marriage: Walter, William, Marjory, and Agnes. Their first home at Washington, now vanished, stood on the south-facing slope below the church, where the Old Hall stands today. Like similar contemporary dwellings, it was probably fortified, with a pele-type tower and other buildings in a courtyard, surrounded by a moat or ditch fed by Washington Beck. To the south, stretching down to the River Wear, lay woodlands where the Washingtons were granted freedom to hunt game.

As tenant of the bishops of Durham, William (and his descendants) held Washington except the church and its lands for an annual rent of £4, was required to attend the bishops' great hunts with two hunting dogs, and had to give one mark to the Common Aid (an occasional tax) when demanded. The great hunt held each autumn in the bishops' park in Weardale was primarily intended to provide meat for the winter. From the first, the Washingtons were attendant upon the prince-bishops as part of their entourage or court.

SIR WALTER DE WESSYNGTON, William's eldest son, had succeeded him before c. 1195. He had married Diana de Dilston, whose marriage settlement, before 1190, included lands in North Milbourne, Northumberland, specified in a deed to which is attached his seal. It bears the device of *a lion passant,* probably deriving from his descent from the earls of Dunbar. He died early and childless.

SIR WILLIAM DE WESSYNGTON II was his younger brother and heir, whose marriage to Alicia de Lexington, a ward of the Crown and the wealthy widow of a Nottinghamshire knight, cost him two palfreys and 60 marks in 1211. This was a large sum at the time and other evidence also suggests his wealth. His name, like that of his father and grandfather, appears among the benefactors of Durham Priory.

SIR WALTER DE WESSYNGTON II, his son and successor, married Lady Joan or Juliana de Ryal sister and heiress of Roger de Whitchester, Keeper of the Rolls in Chancery and Canon of St. Paul's. She brought to the Washington family lands in both Northumberland and County Durham. Her half-uncle was the Cumberland magnate William de Greystoke and later Washingtons held lands in the Greystoke barony. Sir Walter II could afford to settle his father's estate of Offerton, as well as some Northumberland property, on his daughter Isabella on her marriage about 1250.

It was probably Sir Walter II who improved upon his forebears' property at Washington by building a hall, vestiges of which remain in the present Old Hall. Most obvious are the two pointed arches which once led from the screens passage at the west end of the hall to the buttery and pantry (converted into a kitchen in the seventeenth century). In the west wall of the latter, a late medieval wood-mullioned window has replaced a lancet from Sir Walter II's time, part of which is still visible.

Sir Walter II was one of eighty-five knights who fought with Bishop Neville's forces on the barons' side in the rebellion led by Simon de Montfort against Henry III. The rebels were defeated at Northampton, but hostilities continued. The royal army asked for the treaty of peace which was signed at Lewes Priory on 14 May, 1264, bringing victory for the cause of Parliament. Two years later, Lady Juliana was a widow. Perhaps Sir Walter II had been killed in the Battle of Lewes, or in the conflict had suffered severe injuries which led to his death. Lady Juliana was alive in 1278.

SIR WILLIAM DE WESSYNGTON III, his eldest son, succeeded him. William married Margaret de Morville, of Helton Fleckett in the Barony of Appleby, further increasing the Cumbrian properties of the Washingtons. Her forebears included Hugh de Morville, Constable of Scotland and his namesake Hugh, baron of Appleby and Knaresborough, who was one of the assassins of Thomas à Becket. Sir William III died in 1288, leaving Margaret a widow. When her elder brother died childless in 1290, she and her sister became joint heiresses of the Morville estates.

Their eldest son was Walter, continuing the tradition of naming the heir after his grandfather. William, the second son, became keeper of the manor of Wark in Tynedale for the King in 1327, but died childless before 8 August that year, leaving a widow, Elizabeth de Thweng.

Other progeny included Robert I, who in 1292 married Joan de Strickland, heiress of Carnforth in Lancashire. From this marriage were descended the Washingtons of Sulgrave, Northamptonshire.

SIR WALTER DE WESSYNGTON III, eldest son of Sir William III, succeeded to the property in 1287. His activities in Durham and Westmorland are well documented and his attendance on Bishop Bek and his successor Bishop Kellaw at their episcopal castles and manors in Durham and Yorkshire may be traced in detail.

In September, 1304, King Edward I visited Washington on his return journey from the Scottish Border, and transacted business in the area for several days. The accommodation which would be needed for the royal retinue is further evidence for the great establishment formerly at Washington; and the expense of entertaining royalty shows the prosperity of the family.

The following year, the king commanded Sir Walter to conduct three rebellious Scottish ecclesiastics—two bishops and an abbot—from Newcastle to prison in Nottingham, when he would be expected to use his own men as an escort.

His first wife, Alice, died in his lifetime and he married again. He died in 1318 or shortly afterwards, leaving a widow Dionysia, who was living in 1349.

The coat of arms of Sir Walter III is preserved on one of his seals and shown also in Thomas Jenyns's Roll of Arms in the fourteenth century. It is a differenced version of the Dunbar lion: *Argent, a lion rampant Gules, over all a bend compony Argent and Azure.*

SIR WILLIAM DE WESSYNGTON IV was his father's successor, continuing also in the service of the bishops of Durham. Much of his activity was in the Scottish Borders and in 1335 he had custody of various lands in Roxburghshire.

Some time before 1346 he was using a new coat of arms. The device was three bars with two molets in chief, apparently based on the shield of the de Lancasters, barons of Kendal. It is shown in 1390 as *Gules, two bars and three molets in chief Argent.* Soon afterwards the tinctures were reversed to the now familiar: *Argent, two bars and three molets in chief Gules* which descendants and later branches of the family have continued to use.

He was at the Battle of Neville's Cross, near Durham, against an invading Scottish army in October, 1346.

Washington Old Hall, north side. Its former entrance from the village green passed the east end of the church. The arch has since disappeared.

Anonymous nineteenth-century drawing.

Afterwards, he held prisoner three Scottish knights, one of whom died in his custody, and of whose barony, also in Roxburghshire, he became guardian, while the others were transferred to the Tower of London. Later, he seems to have forfeited some of his Scottish lands, for they were restored to him in 1364.

In 1348 he made a settlement of two thirds of Washington on his wife Katherine, who survived him when he died in 1367.

SIR WILLIAM DE WESSYNGTON V was 24 years old when he succeeded to his father's estates in May, 1367. He was to be the last of the main line of the early Washington family. On 10 June, 1369, he was granted royal letters of protection when he was about to leave the realm with the Duke of Lancaster; and he served 'beyond seas' for a year from 21 June, 1373 with Sir Henry de Percy.

At the Battle of Otterburn (the inspiration for the ballad 'Chevy Chase') on 19 August, 1388, he was among the companions of the younger Sir Henry de Percy (Shakespeare's 'Harry Hotspur'), continuing to fight valiantly after Percy's capture until he himself was taken prisoner by the Scots.

He served on the council of Bishop Fordham of Durham until he died in 1399, leaving Alina his wife a widow. His heiress was his only child, Eleanor who, before April 1402, married her kinsman Sir William Tempest of Studley Royal, Yorkshire.

JOHN WESSYNGTON (1371–1451), the famous Prior of Durham, was great-great-nephew of Sir Walter de Wessyngton III. During his lifetime the last of the male line of the original Washingtons died, and Washington itself passed to the Tempest family through the marriage of Eleanor, and subsequently to the Mallorys through her daughter.

John took the monastic habit at Durham in 1390, received priest's orders and was sent immediately to Durham College, Oxford, where he was in residence during the academic year 1394–5 and remained for thirteen years, becoming a Fellow of his college. He served several times as one of its two bursars and was involved in extensive new building there, including the library which is now part of Trinity College. After returning permanently to the mother house at Durham in 1407, he became an efficient Sacrist and Chancellor. Of a scholarly disposition, he collected material for a history of the Benedictine order in Durham; and a manuscript preserved in Durham Cathedral Library contains works he wrote on fifteen different subjects.

He was elected Prior in 1416 and became first of those who were appointed Visitor of all other Benedictine monasteries in England. In his many and wide travels he must have encountered other members of his family.

At Durham he was the greatest repairer the Cathedral has ever known. Especially he is remembered for the rebuilding of a room between the south transept and the chapter house, over the slype or parlour. It was fitted as a library to receive all the books, which he had rebound, from their cupboards in the cloister, which was being rebuilt in his time and where his coat of arms appears, with many others, in the roof.

Among other work in the church itself, he bought a 'pair of organs' to improve the music; and provided a room for the Sacrist, later used as a schoolroom, off the north choir aisle.

When he retired in 1446, having served as Prior for twenty-nine years, he was allowed a handsome pension and allocated a suite of rooms and attendance in his old age. He was buried in Durham Cathedral at the western end of the north aisle of the choir.

On George Washington's birthday, 1944, a plaque to the memory of John Wessyngton was unveiled in the cloister on the wall between the south-west door of the church and the day-stair to the dormitory. It is inscribed: 'REMEMBER IN THESE/CLOISTERS WHICH WERE/FINISHED IN HIS DAY/JOHN WASHINGTON/OF WASHINGTON IN THIS COUNTY/PRIOR OF THE CATHEDRAL CHURCH/1416–1446 WHOSE FAMILY HAS WON/AN EVERLASTING NAME IN LANDS/TO HIM UNKNOWN.'

John Wessyngton's coat of arms appears in Selby Abbey in medieval glass on the south side of the choir clerestory in the second window from the east, doubtless because of Durham's connection with the neighbourhood. Among Yorkshire lands, the Bishop of Durham held Howden; and the Prior and Convent had churches there and at nearby Hemingborough, whose church was raised to collegiate rank during John Wessyngton's tenure of office. Other shields associated with Hemingborough were placed in Selby Abbey church also. The Washington glass was in the fifth clerestory window with three other medieval coats of arms before repairs in 1865.

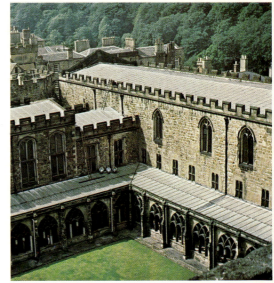

Durham Cathedral: the cloister, with refectory (left). John Wessyngton was a Durham monk from 1390. During his time the cloister was rebuilt with its present roof and the immense dormitory (right) built 1396–1404.

A. W. Robbins.

Durham Cathedral: western towers from the window of the Song School, formerly the library room created by John Wessyngton, Prior 1414–46.

R. W. Billings, 1846.

The Washingtons of Cumbria and Lancashire

ROBERT DE WESSYNGTON I (*c.* 1273–1324), founder of the line which moved to Sulgrave, acquired Tewitfield, half of Carnforth in Warton, Lancashire, on the north-east of Morecambe Bay, by his marriage with Joan de Strickland in 1292. She was sister of Sir Walter de Strickland of Sizergh and, like her husband, could claim Earl Gospatric of Dunbar among her forebears. The Washingtons were tenants of the other half of Carnforth, so that by one title or another they held the whole of the manor. Robert also held other lands in Westmorland.

Sizergh Castle from the south-west: the fourteenth-century pele tower, to which a hall range and other rooms were added later. Among other family documents here is the marriage settlement of 21 September, 1292 of Robert de Wessyngton and Joan, daughter of Sir William Strickland, heiress of Carnforth in Warton, from whom all the Washingtons of Warton are descended. Sizergh, owned by the Stricklands from 1239, was given with 1,560 acres to the National Trust in 1950. It is open to visitors 1 April–31 October, Mon., Wed., Thur., and Sun., 2–5.45 p.m.
Basil Clarke.

With his brother John and other local landowners, he became involved in a controversy over the possession of the rectory of Kendal, which Master Alan de Easingwold, official of Bishop Bek of Durham, had usurped. Through the influence of Master Alan, both Robert and John were excommunicated in 1295; but the Archbishop of York intervened and absolved them both. Master Alan, however, continued to sue Robert and two others for assaults until 1327.

Robert took part in the disastrous Battle of Stirling on 11 September, 1297, acting as esquire to his overlord whose nephew's life he saved. Two years later he was serving once more against the Scots; and on 20 February, 1307, Robert de Wessyngton, Sir Walter de Strickland and two others were appointed Commissioners of Array to muster 500 men at Carlisle by the following Monday to resist Robert Brus.

In February 1300 Sir William de Strickland, Robert's father-in-law, accused Robert of stealing cattle; but family peace must have been restored because, probably through Strickland influence, Robert was returned as M.P. for Westmorland to the Parliament of May 1300.

He was granted guardianship of a minor in 1302 and in return for this service received annually a robe suitable for an esquire and 40 shillings (from rents) at Kendal Castle each Christmas.

There had been family trouble in 1321 when justices appointed a commission to enquire into complaints laid by Sir Walter de Strickland that Robert and John de Wessyngton, with others, had broken into his manor of Sizergh with armed men, wrecking doors and windows of the buildings, assaulting his servants and carrying away his bondman.

Robert continued to be active in local affairs in both Lancashire and Westmorland; and on 9 May, 1324, he was summoned as a principal landowner to attend the Great Council at Westminster on 30 May. Before undertaking the long journey south, he was summoned to serve on a Lancashire jury in an important case. He died before 18 August of the same year.

Burneside Hall, near Kendal. A remarkable surviving example of a fortified house, within a curtain wall 6 feet thick and 70 feet long with a rampart walk 10 feet above ground. The gatehouse, once with two sets of gates, has a porter's lodge above and a guardroom on one side. Within stands a thirteenth-century pele tower; a chapel; and a hall of *c.* 1550, 25 feet long, with massive oak screens, and a long south wing with fine plasterwork *c.* 1600. It was rescued from ruin early this century and is now a private farmhouse.
Basil Clarke.

Troutbeck Park and Windermere. The medieval park (now farmed for the National Trust) where John de Wessyngton and his son poached in 1368, lies north of Troutbeck village where Townend (National Trust), a seventeenth-century farmhouse, is open daily from April to October. For further details, contact the Regional Information Officer at Ambleside. Tel. 0966 33883. (Troutbeck Park is not open.)
Moyna Kemp.

JOHN DE WESSYNGTON, Robert's brother, married Elizabeth de Burneside in 1293. She was the daughter and heiress of Sir Gilbert de Burneside, clerk and Sheriff of Westmorland, and sister of Sir Roger de Burneside, who was M.P. for Westmorland in 1321, 1328 and 1340.

By this marriage, John acquired estates in Asthwaite, Crook and Strickland Ketel, with Hallhead (or Hallad) Hall, near Kendal and Howgill in north Yorkshire, not far distant. John de Wessyngton was made coroner for Westmorland, but deprived of office in 1331.

The next generation differed little from its forebears or contemporaries, for in 1366, Joan de Copeland (widow of Sir John de Copeland who captured King David of Scotland at the Battle of Neville's Cross in 1346) complained that John de Wessyngton, his son John, and others broke into her parks at Troutbeck and elsewhere in Kendale, fished in her fisheries and carried away her deer and timber. Their descendants were the Washingtons of Adwick-le-Street near Doncaster, Yorkshire.

ROBERT DE WESSYNGTON II, eldest son of Robert de Wessyngton I and Joan de Strickland, succeeded his father who died in 1324. When Robert was 16 years old, his parents had settled on him their property in Carnforth in 1312, on his marriage with Agnes le Gentyl, only daughter and heiress of Ranulf le Gentyl. There were three sons of the marriage. Robert, the eldest, born about 1326, was a witness for Sir Robert Grosvenor in 1386 in the famous Scrope-Grosvenor dispute about the coats of arms of these two families. (By his wife, Marjory Haukin, he had an only daughter Agnes de Washington, wife of Edmund Lawrence, whose son Sir Robert Lawrence [b. 1371] inherited Carnforth. Their decendants, the Lords Gerard and Dukes of Hamilton, frequently quartered the Washington coat of arms.) The second son was Edmund; and John was the third and youngest.

JOHN DE WESSYNGTON became heir to his father on his death between 1346 and 1348. In 1363 John married Eleanor (Alina), widow of Sir William de Lancaster of Howgill, Westmorland. She died in 1370. In 1382 he married his second wife Joan, daughter and heiress of John de Croft of Tewitfield in Warton, Lancashire. The present Lady Chapel in Warton church was formerly the

Washington House in Warton main street, a typical yeoman's house, was rebuilt in the eighteenth century, but bears a datestone of 1612 with the initials RWS (probably Richard or Robert Washington and his wife). Many members of the Washington family have lived in the neighbourhood.
Moyna Kemp.

Warton Church (dedicated to St. Oswald, King of Northumbria, d. 650), mother church of Silverdale, Carnforth, Borwick and Yealand, has a plain round twelfth-century font (with elaborately decorated lead lining of 1661). The church was rebuilt, except for the north aisle, in the fifteenth century. Robert Washington (d. 1483) was responsible for the tower. His coat of arms, on its outside north wall, was removed inside in 1955 for preservation.
Basil Clarke.

chantry chapel of the Croft family and an ancient carving of their coat of arms is above the modern north porch. John died in 1407/8 leaving Joan a widow.

JOHN DE WESSYNGTON, son and heir of John de Wessyngton and Joan Croft, was born c. 1385 and inherited the manor of Tewitfield and other lands from his mother in 1408. He died in 1423.

ROBERT WASHINGTON III of Tewitfield, his son and heir, was born about 1420 and married Margaret, widow of John Lambertson of Warton. Warton church was re-built in the fifteenth century except for the north aisle and Robert was responsible for the building of the tower. His coat of arms was carved on a stone on the outside of its north wall. It was removed in 1955 to a corresponding position inside the wall for its better preservation. Robert died on 7 December 1483.

ROBERT WASHINGTON IV of Warton, second son of Robert Washington III and his wife Margaret, was born c. 1455 and became the next heir. He married, firstly, Elizabeth, daughter of John Westfield of Overton, Lancashire; secondly, the daughter of Myles Whittington of Borwick, Lancashire; and thirdly, Agnes Bateman, of Heversham, Westmorland. His will is dated 6 September, 1528, just before his death.

JOHN WASHINGTON of Warton was born about 1478 to Robert Washington IV and his first wife Elizabeth. He married Margaret, daughter of Robert Kytson of Warton and sister of Sir Thomas Kytson (the ancestor of Earl Spencer and Sir Winston Churchill). John died before 1528 in the lifetime of his father and his eldest son, Lawrence, became heir to his grandfather, Robert Washington IV. Lawrence left Warton for Sulgrave about 1530.

The Washingtons of Adwick-le-Street, Yorkshire

Washingtons first appeared in the Doncaster area of Yorkshire in 1552–3. James Washington was the second son of Richard Washington of Grayrigg, near Kendal, a kinsman of Lawrence Washington of Warton (who was born about 1500 and purchased Sulgrave in 1539). James was born in 1535 and inherited from his father, who died in 1555, the Yorkshire estates of Armthorpe and Hampole Priory. Before 1563, James added lands in Arksey, Bentley, Doncaster, Barlby, Rossington, and elsewhere, as well as the manor of Adwick-le-Street, where he built the Hall, an impressive mansion with a five-gabled front, now demolished, which became the chief seat of his descendants.

At the heraldic visitation of 1563–4, James stated that he was "descended owte of the howse of Hallad Hall in Northumberland descended of a third brother of the same howse", a statement repeated in 1612 by his son Richard. Hallad, or Hallhead Hall, near Kendal, was the residence of descendants of John Washington and Elizabeth de Burneside until Henry VIII's reign, when the last male heir died. The mistaken idea that Hallad Hall was in Northumberland may have originated in family oral tradition which referred to that county in connection with the Washingtons of Washington. Hallhead Hall is a farm today.

James, a Cambridge graduate of St. John's College, married Margaret, daughter of John Anlaby of Etton, near Beverley. By her he had twelve children. Four of the sons were also sent to Cambridge University. James was at Adwick during the time of the learned priest Robert Parkyn, who continued there from the reign of Henry VIII to the time of Elizabeth I, and who bequeathed to him a copy of one of John Calvin's works. James Washington became a Justice of the Peace and died at Adwick-le-Street in 1580, aged 44 years. His wife was only 35 years old when she died in 1579.

Their tomb in Adwick-le-Street church lies under one of the arches between the chancel and the south chapel. It is an altar tomb with an alabaster slab incised with the figures of James and his wife Margaret, each bearing a coat of arms of the appropriate family on the breast. The Washington shield has the difference of a star, indicating a third son. The tomb also commemorates their twelve children, seven sons and five daughters, who are named: Bartholomew, Philip, Richard, Martin, Francis, John, Catherine, Jane, Mary, Francis, Lucy and Leonard.

Only two sons survived to marriageable age: Richard, and Bartholomew who became rector of Burghwallis in Yorkshire. Richard, the eldest living at his father's death, became the heir. He married Mary, daughter of Thomas Wombwell, of Wombwell, and had nine children. In 1624–5 he was recorded as Treasurer of the Lame Soldiers.

Darcy, Richard's heir, married Ann, daughter of Matthew Wentworth of Bretton and a kinswoman of the Earl of Strafford, Charles I's favourite. When the Civil War broke out, Darcy's elder sons, another Darcy and James, became officers in the royalist forces and were killed during their father's lifetime. James, a lieutenant-colonel, died in the second seige of Pontefract (Yorkshire) which held out for the King for nine months before surrendering on 21 March, 1649, two months after the death of Charles I.

The younger Darcy was married and had six children, of whom Richard became heir to his grandfather. This Richard married and had five children. He died in 1678, aged 39. His eldest child, another Richard, who was born in 1673, held Adwick when he came of age. He was the last of the line to hold the manor, which was sold to Sir George Cooke. Adwick Hall was demolished in the nineteenth century and its grounds are now a public park.

The Washingtons of Adwick-le-Street are also remembered at the neighbouring church of Adwick-on-Dearne, where their coat of arms is carved on the Jacobean pulpit.

Francis, a younger brother of the last Richard Washington of Adwick-le-Street, became Rector of Sprotborough, and died in 1678. His eldest son Godfrey, born there in 1670, followed his father into the ministry. He distinguished himself at Cambridge, where there is a memorial to him in Peterhouse chapel and another, surmounted by the Washington coat of arms, on the north wall just inside the door of Little St. Mary's, where he was Vicar from 1705–1729.

Francis Washington's cousin James, grandson of the first Darcy Washington, became a merchant in Rotterdam. In a letter of 21 February, 1844, to the American consul at Leipzig, a Baron von Washington stated that his great-grandfather, James Washington "was so deeply involved in the unfortunate affair of the Duke of Monmouth, in the time of Charles II, 1683 and 1684, that he was obliged to flee from England . . . to Holland." The Dutch Washingtons died out in the male line in 1845; but a distinguished German off-shoot of the family in Bavaria and Austria flourished until 1929.

Adwick-le-Street, St. Lawrence: the Elizabethan Washington tomb of freestone. The covering marble slab is incised with the figure of James Washington (1535–1580) in hat and ruff, with sword, and on his breast the arms of Washington with star for difference on the upper bar; and Margaret his wife (d. 1579), daughter of Sir John Anlaby, with the arms of Anlaby (a chevron between three chess-rooks) on her breast. At their feet are their twelve children, named. The church has memorials also to three of their descendants.

Phil Callaghan.

The Washingtons of Sulgrave Manor

Sulgrave Manor, completed by Lawrence Washington about 1560 and owned by descendants until 1659. Parts of the Tudor house, which had formerly a longer frontage, were pulled down before 1700, when the north wing was added. Restoration completed in 1929 included a new wing east of the central porch, replacing the demolished kitchen and buttery. Open to visitors daily except Wednesdays, 1 April–30 September, 10.30 a.m. –5.30 p.m.; 1 October–31 March, 10.30 a.m.–4 p.m. Closed daily 1–2 p.m. Not open in January.

East Midlands Tourist Board.

LAWRENCE WASHINGTON, born *c.* 1500, was the eldest son of John Washington of Warton, Lancashire, and his wife Margaret Kytson. By 1529, Lawrence was bailiff to William, Lord Parr, of Horton in Warton, whose family had inherited the barony of Kendal by that time; and who was uncle to Katherine Parr, sixth wife and ultimately the widow of Henry VIII. In 1530, Lawrence married Elizabeth, the widow of William Gough, a wealthy wool merchant of Northamptonshire, where William Parr also had extensive property. Soon afterwards, he moved to Northampton, where Elizabeth had business interests and a town house, besides other properties. Lawrence swiftly became well established in the wool trade and was Mayor of Northampton in 1532 and again in 1545.

Meantime, Elizabeth died childless and Lawrence married another wealthy widow in 1538: Amy Tomson, third daughter of Robert Pargiter of Greatworth, near Sulgrave, through whom he acquired Sulgrave and Stuchbury. At the dissolution of the monasteries Lawrence (like his relatives at Adwick-le-Street) profited by Henry VIII's policy, for he was able to buy the properties he held as tenant of St. Andrew's Priory, Northampton and which passed to the Crown. He purchased Sulgrave in 1539 for the modest sum of £324 14s. 10d.

Lawrence, increasingly prosperous, and with a growing family—Amy bore him four sons and seven daughters—built Sulgrave Manor house, completing it about 1560. Amy died on 6 October, 1564, but Lawrence survived her for almost twenty years. He died on 19 February, 1584 and was buried in Sulgrave church in front of the Washington family pew, where he and his wife and eleven children are commemorated.

ROBERT WASHINGTON, their eldest son, was born in 1544 and inherited Sulgrave Manor with about 1250 acres. He was married twice: firstly, in 1565 to Elizabeth, daughter and heiress of Walter Light (Lyte) of Radway Grange, Warwickshire, and a descendant of the Villiers family; and secondly to Anne Fisher. All his children were by his first wife. In 1600, Robert bought the manor of Nether Boddington from his son-in-law, Albert Wakelyn. Although he continued to live at Sulgrave, he transferred ownership of the manor house there to his eldest son Lawrence in 1601. Lawrence sold the demesne lands to Thomas Atkins, of Over Winchcombe, Buckinghamshire,

on 20 August, 1605, retaining only the house and seven acres of land. With the consent of his father, Lawrence sold the reversion of the remainder on 1 March, 1610 to his cousin Lawrence Makepeace, son of Robert's sister Mary and Abel Makepeace.

Robert's brother, Lawrence, became Registrar of the Court of Chancery and married firstly, Mary Argall (*née* Scott), widow of Richard Argall, who had died in 1588, leaving five sons and six daughters living. One of the sons was Sir Samuel Argall, who emigrated and was Deputy-Governor of Virginia in 1617–19. On Mary's death in 1605, Lawrence married Martha Nuse. He died in 1619 and is buried at Maidstone. Their son, another Lawrence, was knighted and, like his father, became Registrar of the Court of Chancery. He was the owner of Stonehenge, died in 1643 aged 64, and is buried at Garsdon, Wiltshire. Their daughter Mary married William Horspoole and is buried at Maldon, near Cliveden.

When Robert died in 1619, his second wife, Anne Fisher, continued to live at Sulgrave Manor house until 1625. She was buried at East Haddon, Northamptonshire, on 16 March, 1652. Robert was succeeded by his grandson, John.

LAWRENCE WASHINGTON, born *c.* 1568, eldest son of Robert Washington and Elizabeth (Light), who sold Sulgrave in 1610 in his father's life-time, married on 30 August, 1588, Margaret, daughter of William Butler, of Tyes Hall, Cuckfield, Sussex, from whom his descendants had the right to quarter the Plantagenet coat of arms on their shield. The eldest son, Robert, died young. The second, John, was knighted in 1623 and inherited the property of his grandfather Robert in 1619, his father having died in 1616. Sir John died at Thrapston, Northamptonshire, in 1668, and the coat of arms and eagle crest are all that remains of his tomb in the church. The third son, William, was knighted in 1622. He married Anne, the penniless half-sister of George Villiers, Duke of Buckingham, the favourite of Charles I. (Their son was Colonel Sir Henry Washington, the cavalier hero of the seige of Worcester, and a commander in the royalist army at the Battle of Edgehill in 1642. His sister Elizabeth, the eventual heiress, married William Legge and became the mother of George Legge, the Admiral who was created first Baron Dartmouth.) The fifth son, the Rev. Lawrence Washington was father of John and Lawrence who emigrated to Virginia. The sixth son, Thomas, was page to Charles I when he visited Madrid in 1623. Two daughters, Margaret and Alice, married members of the Sandys family.

Lawrence moved to Little Brington, probably in 1610 (the year Sulgrave Manor was sold) to a house in the village street still known as Washington House. Its date stone is inscribed 1606, and it is said to have been bought by Lord Spencer from Francis Barnard, whose grandson, Sir John Barnard, married Shakespeare's granddaughter. The Spencers, like the Washingtons, had made a fortune in the wool trade and their seat has been at Althorp, near Brington, since 1508. Lawrence, who was third cousin to the first Lord Spencer through his great-grandmother, Margaret Kytson, probably became agent to the Spencers.

Lawrence died on 13 December, 1616, in his father's lifetime, and is buried in Great Brington church in the north aisle. Although the tomb slab has been broken and repaired, the Washington coat of arms, impaled with the arms of his wife, Margaret Butler, is well preserved and a long inscription mentions their eight sons and nine daughters. One of the sons, also Lawrence, was great-

great-grandfather of George Washington.

Lawrence's younger brother, Robert, was already at Great Brington in 1601, when he is recorded as church-warden. He farmed about sixty acres of land and lived in a house at the end of the village, on the right of the road to Whilton running west from the church. A church pew allocation of 1606 shows that Robert Washington and his wife occupied the uppermost pews in the south aisle, the benches on the same side being for his men-servants, John Middleton and Richard Warwicke. Robert died on 10 March, 1622/3 and his wife Elizabeth on 19 March of the same year. Their tomb, with two fine brasses, one bearing the family coat of arms with a crescent for difference (indicating a second son), is in the centre of the nave.

In 1860, Earl Spencer gave facsimilies of both the Washington tombs to the Hon. Charles Sumner, who presented them to the State of Massachusetts, where they were placed in the entrance hall of the State House at Boston.

Great Brington church contains magnificent tombs of the Spencer family in a chapel on the north side of the chancel. In the centre is the tomb of Sir John Spencer, who died in 1586, and his wife who was niece of Margaret Kytson, the mother of Lawrence Washington, the builder of Sulgrave Manor house in the time of their grandson, Sir Robert Spencer, who was created first Baron Spencer in 1603. Lady Diana Spencer, who married Charles, Prince of Wales in 1981, is a descendant of the family.

The Reverend **LAWRENCE WASHINGTON,** fifth son of Lawrence and Margaret Washington, was born in 1602 at Sulgrave. He was educated at Brasenose College, Oxford, where he graduated B.A. in 1623, was a Fellow of the college from 1624–33, proceeded M.A. in 1626, became a Proctor and lector in 1631, and obtained a B.D. degree in 1632.

He became rector of Purleigh, Essex, a wealthy living, in April 1633. That summer he married Amphyllis, daughter and co-heiress of John Twigden, of Little Creaton, North-amptonshire, then living with her mother and stepfather at Tring. Their eldest son John was born the following spring.

Amphyllis' mother Anne had married a Mr. Roades after John Twigden's death; and after being widowed a second time married Andrew Knolinge of Tring as her third husband. Evidently he was fond of his stepdaughter Amphyllis. He became godfather of her second son, another Lawrence, who was baptised at Tring on 18 June, 1635. Of the other five children, two more were baptised at Tring: Elizabeth, on 17 August, 1636, and the youngest, William, baptised on 14 October, 1641. Evidently the family spent a good deal of time there.

In 1643, Parliament ordered the living of Purleigh to be sequestered and the Rev. Lawrence Washington ejected. The Civil War was in progress. He was accused as a "Malignant Royalist" and "oft drunk", but the latter charge was refuted. From this time he was allowed to hold only the very small, poor living of Little Braxted, near Maldon, Essex. He became greatly improverished and Amphyllis and the children made their home with her stepfather at Tring.

When Andrew Knolinge died in January, 1648/9, he left money to his wife's children and grandchildren, the family of Amphyllis Washington: John, William, Elizabeth, Mary and Martha, bequeathing the residue, including property, to his godson Lawrence, who was then only 13 years old. Administration was granted to John Dagnall of Grove, Tring parish, as none of the children was of age. Probably both John and Lawrence attended school in Tring.

Amphyllis pursued the rights of her husband and

Sulgrave, St. James the Less. The fourteenth-century church contains the Washington pew at the east end of the south aisle. Four panels of Elizabethan glass in the adjacent window depict coats of arms of three generations: lower right, Lawrence Washington and his wife Amy Pargiter; lower left, his father John Washington and his wife Margaret Kytson; above, their eldest son Robert and his wife Elizabeth Light. Lawrence and Amy lie buried in front beneath brasses (now damaged) showing their eleven children. Tradition assigns ownership of a medieval chest to the Washingtons. Its origin may be St. Andrew's Priory, Northampton.

Canon S. Brown, Vicar of Sulgrave.

Sulgrave Manor in the nineteenth century. The west wing had gone by 1700 and the house became dilapidated in the eighteenth century.

Anonymous nineteenth-century drawing.

Washington House, Little Brington (7 miles from Northampton) to which Lawrence Washington (1568–1616) and his wife Margaret Butler moved from Sulgrave about 1610.

Anonymous nineteenth-century drawing.

children and in September, 1649, succeeded in obtaining from the Cromwellian Standing Committee for Essex a small income from the living of Purleigh to help her family.

The Rev. Lawrence Washington died in poverty and was buried on 21 January, 1652/3 in the churchyard of All Saints, Maldon, Essex, where the triangular church tower was restored as a Washington memorial, and citizens of Malden, Massachusetts, presented a stained glass window in 1928.

Portrait, dated 1593, of a boy aged 2 years 9 months, long thought to be Sir Henry Washington (hero of the siege of Worcester), but probably his father, Sir William, who was that age in 1593. Small boys of his period and rank wore dresses.

The Earl of Dartmouth.

JOHN WASHINGTON (1633/4–1677), eldest son of the Rev. Lawrence Washington, was about 19 years old, and so under age, when his father died in 1654. Two years later, his mother Amphyllis died intestate and was buried at Tring on 19 January, 1654/5. When John came of age soon afterwards, he went to London, probably taking Lawrence with him.

A year later, on 8 February, 1655/6, John obtained a grant of administration of his mother's estate; and in June 1656 Lawrence came of age and inherited the residue of the estate of his godfather, Andrew Knolinge. With this financial backing, the brothers now turned their attention to new opportunities in trade with the American colonies. Their aunts Margaret and Alice had married into the Sandys family, of which Sir Edwin Sandys had been one of the founders of Virginia.

John, already married, sailed for Virginia later in 1656 as mate and voyage partner of Edward Prescott, owner of the *Sea Horse* of London, a ketch engaged in the tobacco trade. They arrived early in 1657. Having taken tobacco on board near Mattox Creek, they weighed anchor and set sail again, but the ketch sank. During the weeks taken up in refloating her, John became attached to the family of a planter, Lieutenant-Colonel Nathaniel Pope, J.P., of The Cliffs, an early settler on the northern neck of Virginia near the Potomac, between Bridges Creek and Popes Creek in Westmoreland County. When the ketch sailed again, John remained. His wife died and in 1658 he married Pope's daughter, Anne. The wedding present from his father-in-law was a 700 acre estate at Mattox Creek, where their eldest son Lawrence was born in 1659.

About March of that year John's brother Lawrence sailed to join him, probably also in the *Sea Horse,* taking a cargo of supplies. He returned to England in the spring of 1660 to marry, on 26 June, Mary, daughter of Edmund Jones, a prosperous attorney of Luton, near Tring. As a merchant trading with Virginia he settled with Mary at Luton, where a daughter, Mary, was baptised on 22 December, 1663 and a second child Charles on 22 November, 1665. Early in 1666 Lawrence, apparently with Mary and the baby, sailed for Virginia leaving their daughter Mary with her grandparents.

John had bought land at Bridges Creek and settled there in 1664. His wife Anne died in 1669 and he re-married. Eventually he owned over 6,000 acres in Virginia, including the nucleus of the Wakefield and Mount Vernon estates. As a Colonel, he led Virginian forces in the Indian War of 1675. Among civil offices, he was a member of the Virginian House of Burgesses for Westmoreland County. The name of his local Anglican parish was changed to Washington in his honour. He died in 1677, leaving a widow, Frances.

In his will, proved in January, 1677/8, he left his youngest sister Martha £10 to help her emigrate to Virginia, arranged accommodation for a year and maintenance until she settled, and 4,000 lbs. of tobacco, the currency of the colony. Martha sailed the same year, the third of the family to emigrate to Virginia. Shortly afterwards, she married Samuel Hayward, clerk of the County of Stafford.

Lawrence died in the spring of the same year as his brother, 1667, leaving his second wife Joyce (*née* Fleming) with their two babies John and Ann, besides three girls by her previous marriage. Lawrence left to his daughter Mary, then aged 13, his English property which was being administered by her grandfather, Edmund Jones. Mary grew up and married the Rev. Edward Gibson, who became Vicar of Haynes, Bedfordshire, had three boys and three girls, and kept in touch with her Virginian relatives through her aunt, Martha Hayward.

When Martha died in 1697, she left legacies to her two sisters in England, the surviving children of her brothers John and Lawrence, and a small bequest to her great nephew Augustine, the father of George Washington.

LAWRENCE WASHINGTON (1659–1698/9) inherited Mattox Creek Farm from his father. In 1685 he was a member of the Virginia House of Burgesses and in about 1686 married Mildred, daughter and co-heiress of Colonel Augustine Warner, of Warner Hall, Gloucester County, Virginia, Speaker of the House of Burgesses and member of the Governor's Council, whose wife was Mildred, daughter of the Hon. George Reade, Acting Governor of Virginia. Lawrence made his will on 11 March, 1698/9 and died soon after, leaving his wife with three children: John, who was nearly seven, Augustine, aged three, and Mildred, a baby.

The proceeds from his personal estates were to be divided equally between his three children and his wife, Mildred, who was to have the profits of the estates towards their upbringing and keeping them at school. His cousin, John Washington, was one of the executors and held the estates in trust.

The inventory of Lawrence's estate lists as the principal item "Tobacco—33,000 lbs.". Such a quantity represents a whole year's crop. Very probably it was collected by George and Matthias Gale, sons of John Gale of Whitehaven, at that time the principal importers of tobacco. In 1700 George in the *Cumberland* (the largest vessel so far built in Whitehaven) and Matthias in the *Europa* were waiting for the annual convoy to

Whitehaven, St. Nicholas: nave of old church. Built first in 1693, it was rebuilt in 1883, but burnt down in 1971. The porch and tower block, left, form the present church. In the churchyard is the grave of George Washington's grandmother, Mildred Gale (*née* Warner), wife of Lawrence Washington, who married secondly George Gale, and died in 1701. Their baby Mildred and her negro nurse are buried here also.

Basil Clarke.

assemble in the Potomac. Before they sailed, and probably on 16 May, Mildred Washington had taken George Gale as her second husband, and left for England with him, accompanied by her three children and a negro slave.

The registers of St. Nicholas, Whitehaven, record the events of the following months: on 7 January, 1700/1, Jane, the negro servant of George Gale, was baptised; Mildred's baby daughter by George Gale, another Mildred, was baptised on 25 January; Mildred herself died and was buried on 30 January; and Jane was buried on 20 February. The baby Mildred survived.

Mildred Washington had made a legal agreement with John Washington about her marriage to George Gale and entrusted her children's education to her new husband in her will. He obtained boarding places for the boys at Appleby School, where his family knew the headmaster. They remained there for about three years from 1701. When George Gale returned to Virginia alone in 1701–2, he was challenged by Lawrence Washington's executors in a long series of court hearings about the children's custody. They were delivered to their father's cousin, John Washington of Chotank, on 3 September, 1705, the boys having had to leave Appleby School on this account. John Washington, junior, came of age in 1712 and had difficulty in obtaining possession of his father's estates from the remaining executors.

AUGUSTINE WASHINGTON (*c.* 1694–1743), younger brother of John, came of age in 1715 and, with an estate of 1700 acres, married on 20 April that year Jane, the 16 year old heiress of Major Caleb Butler, J.P., of Westmoreland County. Their first child, Butler, died in infancy. Two years after his marriage he purchased a further 150 acres on the bank of the Potomac and in 1722 was preparing to build a new house at Pope's Creek (Wakefield). During these years three other children were born: Lawrence, Augustine and Jane. He continued to acquire agricultural land for tobacco growing and in 1726 or 1727 moved to Pope's Creek. On

26 May that year, his sister Mildred transferred to him the estate of Epsewasson, later called Mount Vernon.

He married secondly, on 6 March, 1730/1, Mary Ball, then an orphan aged 23, only daughter of Colonel Joseph Ball, of Epping Forest, Lancaster County, Virginia, by his second wife Mary Johnson. Their first child, born on 22 February, 1731/2, was George, who became the first President of the United States of America. Subsequently, six other children were born to Augustine and Mary: Elizabeth, Samuel, Charles, John, Augustine, and Mildred who died in infancy.

Lawrence was at Appleby School from 1729 and left for Virginia in 1732, giving half-a-guinea to the school library fund as a leaver. He seems to have returned the same year with his younger brother Augustine (known as Austin) who was at Appleby School from 1732 to 1741. Both boys' names appear on the school honours board. Lawrence spent Christmas 1732 with the Rev. and Mrs. Lawrence Washington of Warton when the former was Vicar of Over Wyresdale nearby; and both boys were at Appleby when their father visited England in 1736 or 1737. Lawrence was probably a schoolboy until 1735, continuing as an usher there until returning to Virginia for good in 1738.

Joseph Deane, Tide Surveyor of the Port of Whitehaven (who lived at 1 Scotch Street from 1730 until moving to 79 Lowther Street in 1746), became a good friend to the boys and corresponded with Lawrence in Virginia from 1738 until at least 1744. Richard Yates, Appleby's headmaster from 1723 to 1781 (fifty-eight years), whose fine memorial is in St. Lawrence church, Appleby, also corresponded with Lawrence and with his father. A letter from Richard Yates to Augustine senior, dated 9 October, 1741 contains the only known reference to the disastrous fire at Little Hunting Creek, the family home.

Lawrence, much admired by his young half-brother George, was nominated Captain in the Virginian forces on 9 June, 1740 and served until December, 1743. Austin stayed on at Appleby until he was almost 21, undoubtedly as an usher for the last three years. He left on 3 December, 1741, also giving half-a-guinea to the school library fund.

Plaque in memory of Mildred Gale, placed in St. Nicholas, Whitehaven, by the Association for the Preservation of Virginia Antiquities in 1955

Basil Clarke.

Appleby Grammar School. The old school attended by two generations of Washington boys was demolished in 1887 and replaced by new buildings.
Wilfred Dodds (based on a nineteenth-century painting).

He arrived home in Virginia on 28 June, 1742, where George now looked forward to his own schooldays at Appleby as intended by his father. His hopes were not fulfilled, for Augustine senior died at Ferry Farm on 12 April, 1743, leaving a widow and five children, of whom George was the eldest and only 11 years old.

Augustine's will left everything on Little Hunting Creek to Lawrence, where he began to build the house called Mount Vernon; Austin received all the Westmoreland property; while to George was bequeathed Ferry Farm. The residue was divided between his widow, Mary, and their own four sons, giving George sufficient means to start as a planter. Meantime, Mary and her children continued to live at Ferry Farm.

Lawrence, promoted to Major and then Adjutant General of the Colony, was now George's hero. He married in 1743 Anne Fairfax, daughter of Colonel William Fairfax, one of a leading Virginia family; and Austin married Anne Aylett soon afterwards. The brothers both seem to have influenced and helped George who, after leaving school, spent some time with Lawrence until February 1747/8 before setting out from Mount Vernon with George William Fairfax on a survey of the South Branch of the Potomac.

Although there were no more visits, the connection with the north of England was not yet over.

George inherited Mount Vernon, the house on Little Hunting Creek Plantation, when Lawrence died in 1752. In 1773 he planned additions at each end and the piazza was erected in 1777. As there was difficulty in obtaining suitable material for the floor, George Washington wrote in July 1784 to George Rumney, a merchant ship-owner of Whitehaven, enquiring for equal quantities of best black and white Whitehaven flagstones, 2½ inches thick and one foot square. The flagstones, from a quarry at St. Bees, were imported and laid in 1786. When renewal was needed in 1914, 1,500 flagstones of the same shape and size were supplied from the same St. Bees quarry near Whitehaven.

George, as General Washington, continued to be interested in Appleby School and Westmorland. On 18 October, 1786, at the capitulation of Yorktown, a frigate surrendered with the town. In answer to a question from the General, its Captain, Hugh Robinson, said he was from "Appleby in Westmorland". The General replied, "I am very glad to meet a Westmorland man; my family sprang from that County, and my brother was at Appleby

School". Hugh's elder brother, the notorious "Jack Robinson" named by Sheridan, was M.P. for Westmorland 1764–1774, then for Harwich until his death in 1802. He was at Appleby School from 1736 to 1744 and therefore a contemporary of both Lawrence and Austin.

YORK became the home of Roger and Mary Morris, whose earlier lives had been intertwined with that of George Washington. In the campaign against the French and Indians in 1755, George, a young colonel in the Virginian militia, was one of three aides-de-camp of General Braddock. George narrowly escaped with his life, but helped his companion, the wounded Captain Roger Morris.

The following February he visited another fellow officer, Beverley Robinson, at New York, whose sister-in-law, the heiress Mary Philipse, was staying there at the time. George was so much attracted by Mary's charms that he was reluctant to leave. A family tradition says that he proposed to her. Certainly Colonel Robinson wrote after his departure pressing his speedy return, as Captain Roger Morris was pressing his own suit.

Mary became Mrs Morris in January, 1758. At the wedding banquet a tall Indian wrapped in a scarlet blanket appeared in the doorway, solemnly pronouncing "Your possessions shall pass from you when the Eagle shall despoil the Lion of his mane." Then he disappeared. The forecast was fulfilled in 1783–4.

Roger took his bride to his newly built mansion on Manhattan Island, where they had two sons and two daughters and where he lived on retiring from the army in 1764. Twenty years later, General Washington visited the family on his way to take command of the American Army before Boston and was graciously received. Roger

York, St. Saviour: memorial to Roger and Mary Morris and their daughter Maria. Mary (*née* Philipse), was courted by George Washington in 1756. She and her husband, loyal to the mother country, had to flee to England in 1783 and lived in York until their death. St. Saviour's is now used by the York Archaeological Trust and is open to visitors.

York Archaeological Trust